INTRODUCTION

Uganda is extraordinarily diverse in natural resources. Within its borders are fresh water lakes, waterfalls, elevated plains, swamps, arid depressions, high snow-capped mountains, forests, woodland and grassland, all supporting an incredible range of plant and animal life.

The remarkable diversity is demonstrated within its animal kingdom where the country ranks among the top ten in the world in terms of the diversity of its mammal groups. It is, in fact, second in Africa and 9th in the world in mammal species and bird life (the country is home to half of Africa's bird species!).

As yet untouched by mass tourism, Uganda's parks and reserves are ideal retreats for the discerning tourist. The experience is very different to that in some of the parks in the region for there are no tarmac roads through the parks, no mass convergence of zebra-camouflaged safari trucks and no animals turning up by appointment! The experience takes you back to basics where patience and good game tracking skills are key.

Half of the world's remaining mountain gorilla population (630) is in Uganda, with 330 in Bwindi Impenetrable National Park in south western Uganda, and the rest in Mgahinga Gorilla National Park at the border with Rwanda and DR Congo.

In order to preserve Uganda's abundant wildlife, protected areas have been set aside over time to ensure the preservation of the country's unique flora and fauna. Protected areas came into being during Uganda's colonial days when large areas of land became uninhabitable due to tsetse fly invasion. These areas were then gazetted for wildlife conservation.

These were Queen Elizabeth National Park, Murchison Falls National Park and Kidepo Valley National Park which were declared protected areas in 1952. Today the country has ten national parks and several wildlife reserves. They include: Queen Elizabeth National Park, Murchison Falls National Park, Kidepo Valley National Park, Kibale Forest National Park, Lake Mburo National Park, Semliki Valley National Park, Bwindi Impenetrable Forest National Park, Mgahinga Gorilla National Park, Mt Elgon National Park and Rwenzori Mountains National Park.

There is also a wildlife education centre in Entebbe, formerly the zoo that offers a good opportunity to view many of the animals in Uganda in a semi-natural environment.

The most visible game in Uganda's national parks is of course the big five i.e. lion, leopard, elephant, rhino and buffalo, plus other tropical African species like Zebra, giraffe, hippo, crocodile, etc. All these animals make Uganda's wildlife a living testimony of the diversity of nature.

CONTENTS

BABOON
Papio anubis

Apart from humans, baboons are the most adaptable of the ground-dwelling primates. All they require of any habitat is water and a safe sleeping place in either tall trees or on cliff faces.

Habits: They sleep, travel, feed and socialise in groups of about 50 individuals, consisting of males and twice as many female plus their young.
Diet: Primarily grass, seeds, leaves and roots. Also eat fruits, insects, small fish, birds and vervet monkeys.
Gestation: Six months.
Lifespan: 30 years.
Population: 1,025 (in the Murchison Falls conservation area alone).

Mainly found in Lake Mburo and Kibale national parks, Budongo and Busitema forest reserves.

BLACK-AND-WHITE COLOBUS MONKEY
Colobus guereza

Perhaps the most common and widely spread forest monkey in Uganda, it is beautifully marked with a black body, white facial markings and a long white tail.

Habits: It lives in small groups, but most spectacular about it is its high jumping skills and the attractive view of its white tail streaming behind.

Diet: Eats fruits as well as nuts, seeds, insects, small vertebrates, leaves, stems, bark, flowers, buds, shoots, fruits and some aquatic plants.

Gestation: 6–7 months

Lifespan: 20 years.

They are found in most national parks and forests.

BLUE MONKEY
Cercopithecus mitis

Despite its name, the Blue Monkey is not noticeably blue: it has little hair on its face, and this does sometimes give a blue appearance, but it never has the vivid blue appearance of a mandrill, for example. Their fur is short, and mainly a grizzled brown colour apart from the face and the mantle, which varies between subspecies. Typical sizes are from 50 to 65 cm in length (not including the tail, which is almost as long as the rest of the animal), with females weighing a little over 4 kg and males up to 8 kg.

Habits: Blue monkeys live in groups that range from 10 to 40 individuals, containing only a single adult male. It is often found in groups with other species of monkeys such as the Red-Tailed Monkey and various Red Colobus monkeys. This is probably for added protection against predators. This monkey prefers to live in tall trees which provide both food and shelter.

Diet: Mainly fruits and leaves. In addition, Blue monkeys tend to concentrate their invertebrate feeding on slow-moving slugs and worms.

Lifespan: Maximum lifespan is probably around 20 years.

Gestation: The female Blue monkey gives birth to a single offspring following a gestation period of five months. Both male and female reach sexual maturity at three years old.

The Blue Monkey is mostly found in rain forests and montane bamboo forests of Kiibale and Mgahinga national parks in western Uganda. There is a population of a subspecies, the golden monkey, which relies heavily on bamboo for nutrition, in Mgahinga N.P.

CHIMPANZEE
Pan troglodytes

Chimpanzees are the mammal most like man. They share more DNA with man than with gorillas! Chimps touch each other a great deal and may even kiss when they meet. An adult chimp often has a special 'friend' with which it spends a lot of time.

Habits: Among the noisiest and most intelligent of wild animals. Spend equal time on land and in trees, do most of their feeding and sleeping in trees. Live in troops of 30 to 80 individuals.

Diet: Fruits, leaves, and occasionally eat meat; they hunt and eat blue, red-tailed and colobus monkeys.

Gestation: 8 months after which they give birth to just one baby. Sexual maturity reached between 8 and 10 years.

Lifespan: 50 years.

Population: 5,000

Mainly found in Semiliki, Kibale and Queen Elizabeth national parks (Kyambura gorge), Budongo, Maramagambo and Kasyoha forests.

DE BRAZZA'S MONKEY
Cercopithecus neglectus

It has a hairy face, a reddish-brown patch around its eyes, white band across its brow, white moustache and beard with a relatively short tail.

Habits: They are active during the morning and afternoon. They are good climbers and swimmers, and run well on the ground.

Diet: It mainly feeds on leaves, shoots, fruit, berries, roots, lizards, insects and geckos.

Gestation: 5 ½ months, giving birth to one infant.

Lifespan: 20 years.

It is seen around Mount Elgon and Semliki national parks.

GREY-CHEEKED MANGABEY
Lophocebus albigena

Mangabey refers to three different genera of old world monkeys: the white lidded mangabey, crested mangabey and highland mangabey. This slender but powerful primate is characterised by its large cheeks and short furry tail that is stiff and held at an acute angle. Weighing up to 12kg, the length of body is approximately 65cm, with the tail adding another 70cm to overall length.

Habits: They live in groups of up to 30 individuals. They make a variety of sounds, including grunts and barks. Male mangabeys make loud calls called woop-gobbles (Woooop!...huhuhuhuhuhuhu).

Diet: Their diet consists of fruits, leaves, flowers, bark and insects.

Gestation: Males reach sexual maturity at 5-7 years. The gestation period is known to be between 164-175 days when a single young is born.

Lifespan: In captivity they can live up to 32 years.

They are mostly found in Kibale Forest National Park.

L'HOEST'S MONKEY
Cercopithecus l'hoesti

It has a black face with backward projecting white whiskers partially covering its ears and carries its tail in an upright position.

Habits: They live in small troops of a dozen. This type of monkey is very hard to see basically because it prefers very dense forests.
A favourite activity is mutual grooming of fur particularly on the chin, cheeks and nape.
Diet: Leaves, shoots, fruit, grass, lichens, occasionally insects and cultivated crops.
Gestation: They have a 5 months' gestation, giving one offspring
Lifespan: Up to 16 ½ years in captivity.

In Uganda, it is more likely to be seen in Maramagambo forest, Kibale forest, Bwindi forest and Queen Elizabeth National Park.

MOUNTAIN GORILLA
Gorilla gorilla

Only about 720 mountain gorillas remain in the world. Gorillas are humble and rarely attack humans. But in an encounter, a person should stay still and refrain from staring or pointing at the gorilla.

Habits: Gorillas live in close-knit family groups that may have up to 30 members.

Diet: Purely vegetarian; mainly leaves, buds, shoots, tubers, roots, stalks, bark, fruits, ferns, etc.

Gestation: 8-10 months. They give birth for the first time at 10 years and will have more offspring every three or four years.

Lifespan: 50 years in wild, gorillas can live up to 50 years whereas in captivity they may live less than 35 years.

Population: 720

Only found in the Bwindi Impenetrable National Park in Uganda (340) and Mgahinga National Park in the Virunga Volcanoes (380) that form part of the Uganda, DR Congo and Rwanda border.

PATAS MONKEY
Erythrocebus patas

It has a lankier build; a light reddish brown coat and a black stripe above the eyes but could easily be confused with the Vervet monkey.

Habits: Their main activity is in the morning and late afternoon. During the midday heat, they rest in the shade together. They are almost terrestrial only sleeping in trees at night.

Diet: Mainly consists of fruit, seeds, leaves, roots, groundnuts, birds, eggs and mineral impregnated earth.

Gestation: 5–6 months, most births occur December – February.

Lifespan: 8 years.

These monkeys are restricted to the dry savannah in Kidepo and the woodlands of northern Uganda.

RED COLOBUS MONKEY
Procobus badius

With a slightly tufted crown, the red colobus monkeys are sociable and usually live in scattered groups of 50 or more animals.

Habits: Their feeding periods are mainly in the morning and afternoon with short midday rests. They are powerful jumpers moving from one tree to anther.

Diet: Largely feed on flowers, shoots, soft fruits and leaves.

Gestation: They have a gestation period of 5-7 months.

Lifespan: Only 2 years, 20 years in the wild.

These are largely restricted to Kibale Forest National Park especially around Bigodi Wetland sanctuary and a few of them in Semliki National Park.

RED-TAILED MONKEY
Cercopithecus ascarius

They have a brownish colour, white whiskers, and a coppery tail with a heart-shaped patch on the nose.

Habits: They usually move in small pairs, associate with other monkeys and can accumulate in-groups of up to 200.

Diet: Like most monkeys, they feed on leaves, flowers and fruits.

Gestation: 5 months.

Lifespan: 16 years.

These monkeys are usually in Kibale forest, Bwindi forest, Mpanga Forest Reserve and Budongo, and Semliki and Queen Elizabeth national parks.

VERVET MONKEY
Cercopithecus aethiops

This has a black face with very distinctive blue male genitals.

Habits: Vervet monkeys live in complex but stable social troops of 10 to 50 individuals mainly consisting of adult females and their immature offspring. Males move freely in and out of these groups. Close social bonds with female relatives begin to develop in infancy, relationships thought to endure throughout life. They are diurnal, sleeping and eating in trees from which they seldom venture.

Diet: Leaves, young shoots, bark, flowers, fruit, bulbs, roots, grass seeds, insects, eggs, baby birds and sometimes rodents and hares. Vervets rarely drink water.

Gestation: 5 ½ months, gives birth to one infant, suckled for 4 months.

Lifespan: 24 years in captivity

They are seen around Mount Elgon and Lake Mburo National parks

BUFFALO
Syncerus caffer

The African Buffalo is a member of the 'Big Five' group of animals that include elephant, rhino, lion and leopard. It is unpredictable and can be dangerous if wounded. In fact, buffalo kill more people in Africa than lions do. Buffaloes are usually calm if left alone.

Habits: Live close to water bodies in herds of a few hundreds. Females and offspring make up bulk of herd. They have poor ability to regulate body temperature so they remain in shade in the heat of day or wallow in mud.

Diet: Grass forms the greatest part of the savannah buffalo's diet. Buffaloes feed more at night than during the day.

Gestation: 12 months. Females have their first calves at 5 years.

Lifespan: 22 to 25 years.

Population: Approx. 22,031

Mainly found in Lake Mburo, Murchison Falls, Kidepo Valley, Kibale and Queen Elizabeth National Parks in western Uganda.

ELEPHANT
Loxodonta africana

The African Elephant is the largest living land mammal. An adult elephant is 3.5m high and weighs over 6,000kgs. Its trunk is remarkable: it serves as a nose, a hand, an extra foot and a tool for gathering food or caressing a companion.

Habits: Generally sociable and form small family groups consisting of an older matriarch and three to four offspring, along with their young.
Diet: Can live in nearly any habitat that has adequate quantities of grass and water. Diet consists of grass, leaves, twigs, bark, fruit and seedpods.
Gestation: 22 months. Usually gives birth to one offspring.
Lifespan: 70 years.
Population: 2,680

Mostly found in Murchison Falls, Queen Elizabeth, Semliki, Kibale, Kidepo Valley and Mount Elgon national parks.

GIRAFFE
Giraffa camelorpardalis

Giraffes are the tallest animals reaching up to 18 feet in height. When startled, a giraffe can gallop at speeds up to 56mph. Because giraffes have a good sense of smell and vision, other animals stay close to them, since they can see predators from afar.

Habits: Has one of the shortest sleep requirements of any mammal; 20 minutes to two hours in a 24-hour period. To avoid predators, giraffes sleep while standing up.

Diet: Leaves and shrubs. A giraffe can eat 60kgs of leaves and twigs daily and can go for a month without drinking because of vulnerable position they must assume in order to drink. This is the reason they do not graze on grass.

Gestation: 15 months. Sexual maturity at 3 – 4 years.

Lifespan: 20 years.

Population: 256

Found in the northern part of Murchison Falls and in Kidepo Valley National Parks.

HIPPOPOTAMUS
Hippoptamus amphibius

The great African Hippopotamus is second in weight only to the elephant; weighing up to 5 tons. The hippo has no sweat glands but has unique glands that produce a red fluid, hence the myth that hippos 'sweat blood.

Habits: Spends most of the day in water to keep cool and minimize heat loss, coming out at night to graze. Usually in herds of 10 or more headed by a dominant male. A hippo can stay under water for up to 5 minutes and often walks along the bottom of lakes.

Diet: Short grass and other plants. Due to their sedentary life, hippos have modest appetites – 40-60kg at each meal.

Gestation: 8 months. Males reach sexual maturity at 7 years (though do not usually breed until age 20) while females at 9 years.

Lifespan: 50 years.

Population: 7,128

Mainly found in Lake Mburo, Queen Elizabeth and Murchison Falls National Parks, Kafu basin and River Nile.

RHINOCEROS
Ceratotherium simum

It is a large, primitive-looking mammal. Because due to its poor eyesight is poor, a Rhino will sometimes charge without apparent reason. Its sense of smell and hearing is very good.

Habits: Rhinos mainly leave alone; the closest rhino relationship is between a female and her calf, lasting 2 – 4 years.

Diet: Rhinos are herbivores, feeding on leaves, buds, and shoots of plants.

Gestation: 15 – 16 months, giving birth to 1 – 6 cubs.

Lifespan: 40 years.

Population: 6 white rhinos

Rhinos had been poached to the point of extinction in Uganda. Only recently re-introduced; kept at Zziwa Ranch in Nakasongola and UWEC.

BUSHBUCK
Tragelaphus scriptus

Bushbucks are forest-edge antelopes. Like leopards, they are solitary animals and usually go out of their way to avoid contact with each other. Most group associations, except for a female and her latest young, are very temporary and only last a few hours or days.

Habits: Bushbucks are almost entirely nocturnal in areas where they may be disturbed during the day.
Diet: Feed mainly on leaves, twigs, flowers and occasionally eat fresh grass.
Gestation: 6 months.
Lifespan: 13 years.
Population: 29

They are found in Katonga Wildlife Reserve, Kafu basin, Lake Mburo National Park and Kibale National Park.

ELAND
Taurotragus oryx

The cow-like eland is the world's largest yet slowest antelope. Because elands are docile, have rich milk and tasty meat, their predators are mainly humans who hunt them for food.

Habits: The older the male, the more solitary its tendencies, while younger animals may form small groups. Males are also more sedentary than females. Calves spend a lot of time grooming and licking each other, developing bonds even stronger than those of a calf with its mother.

Diet: Elands feed on shrubs, leaves, fruits and tuberous roots.
Gestation: 8-9 months usually giving birth to one calf. Female elands reach sexual maturity at 2.5 months.
Lifespan: 25 years.
Population: 619
Mainly found in Lake Mburo and Kidepo Valley national park.

IMPALA
Aepytceros melampus

The Impala – a member of the antelope family – is handsome, graceful, and slender with a chestnut colouring and sleek appearance. Impalas were so common in Kampala (Uganda's capital) that the city's was named after them i.e. kasozi ka impala (hill of impala).

Habits: The females form herds of 10 to 50 and wander in and out of male territories. Bachelor males are allowed to remain in male territories if they ignore the females.
Diet: Impalas eat tender young grass shoots in the wet season and herbs and shrubs at other times. During the dry season they must drink daily.
Gestation: 7 months.
Lifespan: 12 years.
Population: 3,300

Found mainly in Murchison Falls National Park, Lake Mburo National Park and Katonga Wildlife Reserve.

GRANT'S GAZELLE
Gazella granti

The largest of the gazelles with tan upper body and white belly. Males are the size of an impala and have powerfully developed necks and long, diverging horns. Grant's gazelles are especially fond of open grass plains, and although they frequent bushy savannas, they avoid areas of high grass.

Habits: Mature males establish territories they may hold as long as eight months. A male tries to detain the female herds of 10 to 25 individuals as they pass through these territories. Grant's gazelles have developed several ritualized postures. For example, the territorial male stretches and squats in an exaggerated manner while urinating and dropping dung, apparently to warn other males to stay away.

Diet: They eat herbs, foliage from shrubs, short grasses and shoots. Not restricted to certain habitats by a dependency on water, they obtain the moisture they need from their food.

Gestation: 6½ months
Lifespan: 10-12 years

They are only found in Kidepo Valley National Park.

GREATER KUDU
Tragelaphus strepsiceros

The second tallest antelope after the eland, with a distinct hump at the shoulder and a coat marked with up to ten narrow white body stripes. Males have a long neck mane and beautiful spirally twisted horns.

Habits: Kudu are most commonly seen in small groups of four to six cows and calves, and separate herd of bachelor of three to five males. They feed at night, early morning and evening, resting during hotter hours of day. They are very agile and can jump a 2.4m (8ft) fence blocking their path.
Diet: They eat leaves, shoots, flowers of a variety of plants, and some grass. They can do without water by feeding on succulent plants.
Gestation: 7 months
Lifespan: 8 – 12 years

Their numbers are very low in Uganda. They can be seen only in Mt Elgon National Park and Kidepo Valley National Park.

GUENTHER'S DIK-DIK
Madoqua kirkii

A dwarf antelope only slightly larger than a hare, with a very reduced tail. The coat is greyish brown with an orangey wash and dark flecks. Males have small, spiky horns while females are without horns and slightly larger than males.

Habits: Dik-dik are active at dawn and dusk. They live in monogamous pairs and are usually accompanied by the latest calf and sometimes also by the previous year's offspring. They live in the same territory for years and avoid predators by concealing themselves in the bushes and remaining motionless.

Diet: They generally eat leaves, shoots, herbs, flowers, seeds and fruit, often times standing on their hind legs. They are completely independent of water, obtaining moisture from their food.

Gestation: 6 months

Lifespan: 10 years

Guenther's dik-dik are only found in north-eastern Uganda – Kidepo Valley National Park and Pian Upe Game Reserve.

HARTEBEEST
Alcelaphus buselaphus

The hartebeest species found in Uganda is known as the Jackson's Hartebeest.
It is one of the fastest antelopes and most enduring runners. These qualities gave rise to the name "hartebeest," which means tough ox.

Habits: It is one of the most sedentary antelopes; making it easy to hunt. Adult females do not form permanent associations with other adults; instead, they are often accompanied by up to four generations of their young.

Diet: Feeds almost entirely on grass, but is not very selective and quite tolerant of poor-quality food.

Gestation: 8 months

Lifespan: 12-15 years.

Population: 4,439

Frequently seen in the Ishasha sector of the Queen Elizabeth National Park, Murchison Falls, Lake Mburo and Kidepo Valley National parks.

KLIPSPRINGER
Oreotragus oreotragus

They are small, chunky-looking antelopes, characteristically seen standing on rock outcrops. Their coat is a greyish yellow-brown with black speckling. Only males have horns which are short and spiky. They are almost twice the size of dik-dik. Females are larger than males.

Habits: Diurnal and partly nocturnal, they are usually seen in pairs sometimes accompanied by calf (which may remain hidden). They pair for life. Klipspringers are commonly seen standing motionless on rocky outcrops.

Diet: Feed on leaves and shoots of shrubs and bushes, fruit and flowers as well as some grass during rainy season.

Gestation: 7 months

Lifespan: 10–12 years

Found mostly in the Kidepo Valley and Lake Mburo National parks.

ORIBI
Ourebia ourebi

The oribi is a small antelope, superficially similar to the reedbuck. It has a reddish brown or yellowish brown coat and a distinctive, short, fluffy, black tail. Males have short, slender, upright horns while females lack horns and are slightly larger and heavier than males.

Habits: Active during the mornings and later afternoons, oribi are solitary or live in pairs, accompanied by one or more offspring. Young males are chased from the territory by their fathers while female are allowed to stay until almost fully grown.

Diet: They prefer green grass but also feed on foliage and herbs during the dry season. They can go without water, getting all the moisture from vegetation.
Gestation: 6 – 7 months
Lifespan: 10 years

They can be found mostly in Murchison Falls National Park.

SITATUNGA
Tragelaphus spekii

Quite similar to the bushbuck, the Sitatunga is shy and retiring. It is semi-aquatic, spending a considerable part of its life in swampy terrain.

Habits: They live in small herds of up to 6 individuals consisting of an adult male with several females and juveniles. They are active throughout the day and night, resting during the hottest hours of the day.

Diet: Grass eaters feeding primarily on fresh sprouting tips of reeds and bull-rushes, aquatic plants and grasses from shallower water.

Gestation: 7½ months and give birth to a single calf.

Lifespan: 19 years.

Found in all the six national parks of Uganda but likely to be seen around the Katonga Wildlife Reserve and around Lake Victoria.

TOPI
Damaliscus lunatus

The Topi is a medium-sized antelope with a striking reddish-brown to purplish-red coat that is glossy, even shiny in bright sunlight.

Habits: Topis are exceptionally social and live in herds of 15 to 20, although in some places, it is possible to see herds of hundreds. Topis are most active in the morning and evening, resting in shade through the hot hours.

Diet: Topis eat only grass, avoiding both mature leaves and very young shoots.

Gestation: 8 months. Females reach maturity at about one and half years, males at about 3 years.

Lifespan: 15 years.

Population: 2,123

Mostly found in Queen Elizabeth and Lake Mburo National Parks.

UGANDA KOB
Kobus kob

This is Uganda's national animal. It is related to the waterbuck and the reedbuck but reddish-brown in colour and bulkier in appearance.

Habits:
Diet: Kobs are herbivores and feed mainly on leaves and reeds.
Gestation: 9 months, giving birth to a single calf.
Lifespan: 17 years.
Population: 30,456

Often seen in Queen Elizabeth, Murchison Falls and Kidepo Valley national parks and also present in Semliki and Katonga wild reserves and Kafu basin.

WATERBUCK
Kobus ellipsiprymnus

Despite its name, the waterbuck is not truly aquatic though it takes refuge there to escape predators. It however inhabits areas that are close to water.

Habits: Generally a quiet, sedentary animal. The male does not mark his territory, as his presence and smell are sufficient. Males often form all-male groups near the occupied territories, while the females stay in their mother's group.

Diet: They mainly feed on grass and other vegetation. Waterbucks feed in the mornings and at night and rest the remainder of the time.

Gestation: 9 months.

Lifespan: 18 years.

Population: 5,771

Mainly found in Lake Mburo and Queen Elizabeth national parks, Kafu River basins and Katonga Wildlife Reserve

ZEBRA
Equus burchelli

No two zebras have the same black and white stripe pattern. Zebras are avid grazers always in constant search of green pastures.

Habits: Family groups are stable with members maintaining strong bonds over the years. Male foals leave their group at ages one to four to join an all-male bachelor group until they are strong enough to head a family

Diet: Grass, leaves and tree bark. Drink regularly; can't go for more than three days without water.

Gestation: 12 months, single foal is born.

Lifespan: Up to 40 years in captivity.

Population: 4,374

Found in Lake Mburo National Park and Kidepo National Park.

CHEETAH
Acinonyx jubatus

Cheetahs are easily distinguishable from leopards by the distinct 'tearmarks' running from inner corners of their eyes to the edges of their mouths. The cheetah is the fastest mammal on earth; it can run at a maximum speed of 70mph (112kph) and has a stride of 23ft (7m) when running flat out.

Habits: It is basically a solitary animal. At times, a male will accompany a female for a short while after mating, but more often the female is alone or with her cubs. The cheetah usually hunts during the first hours of morning and the last hours of evening, but is also active on moonlit nights.

Diet: They are carnivores, hunting medium-sized and small antelopes particularly gazelles and impalas, young wildebeest and topi, warthog piglets, hares and occasionally zebra foals.

Gestation: 3 months
Lifespan: 10 – 12 years

Cheetahs are becoming extinct in Uganda due to shrinking habitat, loss of species to prey upon, disease and a high rate of cub mortality. They are only found in Kidepo Valley National Park.

LEOPARD
Panthera pardus

The leopard is secretive, elusive, shrewd and a cunning, stealthy hunter. Leopards are basically solitary and go out of their way to avoid one another.

Habits: Leopards are primarily nocturnal, usually resting during the daytime.
Diet: They mainly prey on fish, reptiles, birds, rodents, hares, hyraxes, warthogs, antelopes, monkeys and baboons.
Gestation: 2 months; usually gives birth to two or three cubs.
Lifespan: 21 years.
Population: 2,843

They are can be found in almost all national parks in the country.

LION
Panthera leo

One of Africa's 'big five', the lion is the largest member of the cat family. They are the top predator in any African ecosystem where they live. Lions have a mane while the lionesses do not.

Habits: Lions are 'social' cats that live in prides of 5-15. Lionesses live with the pride for life, while the lions leave the pride of birth at ages 2 – 4. Passing lions of the same pride greet each other by rubbing their cheeks together.

Diet: Lions hunt at night and their typical diet includes zebra, giraffe, buffalo, gazelles and impala.

Gestation: 110 days (just under four months), give birth to up to four cubs.

Lifespan: 12-16 years in the wild, 25 years in captivity.

Population: 575

They are mainly found in Murchison Falls, Queen Elizabeth and Kidepo Valley national parks.

SERVAL
Felis serval

The Serval is a slender long legged cat. It is a very agile and graceful cat with a light tawny colour with solid black spots (like a cheetah), and white undersides. It is often described as a small Cheetah.

Habits: Elusive and shy, servals are for the most part nocturnal, hunting by sight and sound more than scent.

Diet: Preys on birds such as guinea fowl, rodents, small mammals, fish and reptiles like snakes and lizards, and invertebrates. Though they will sometimes raid farms and take poultry.

Gestation: 70-75 days, gives birth to 2-3 young usually during rainy season.

Lifespan: 20 years.

They are mainly found in Kibale National Park.

JACKAL
Cerus adustus

A member of the dog family, the jackal looks more like a fox. In Uganda, we have mostly the side-stripped and black-backed jackals.

Habits: Usually hunts alone, preferring to hunt at night; it begins its hunt at sunset and ends at sunrise. A mating pair of jackals often stays together for years – sometimes for life. Male and female care for puppies.

Diet: Chiefly a scavenger; feeds on the remains of dead animals, but will occasionally hunt down small mammals like lizards, insects, and also eats grass.

Gestation: 2 months, giving birth to 3-6 puppies.

Lifespan: Jackals have a lifespan of 10-14 years.

Mainly found in Kidepo Valley, Bwindi and Mgahinga national parks.

HUNTING DOG (WILD DOG)
Lycaon pictus

Hunting dogs (or wild dogs as they are also known) are medium-sized, dog-like carnivores with large bat ears and a white-tipped tail. Their scientific name means painted or ornate wolf, aptly describing their distinctive tri-coloured coat markings of yellow, dark brown and white. Each animal has a unique coat colour and can be individually recognised.

Habits: They are diurnal (active during the daytime) pack-hunting predators, hunting at dawn and dusk. Their basic lifestyle is that of nomadic wanderers ranging over vast areas in search of prey. They are highly social, with packs of 20 to 40 dogs. Each pack is led by a male and female known as the dominant or alpha pair.
Diet: They usually hunt animals the size of gazelles and impalas as well as Cape hares and dik-diks.
Gestation: 2½ months giving birth to 5-12 puppies.
Lifespan: 10 years.

Wild dogs are on the endangered species list. It is estimated that there are between 3,000 - 5,000 individual wild dogs in about 600-1,000 packs remaining in Africa. They can be sighted in Queen Elizabeth National Park.

HYENA
Crocuta crocuta

Thought to be timid, the hyena can be bold and dangerous, attacking animals and humans. Unlike most animals, the female spotted hyenas are dominant over the males.

Habits: Hyenas are organised into clans of related individuals and they mark their territories by depositing a strong-smelling substance along the boundaries.

Diet: Various animals, bones, vegetables and other animals' droppings. Although they eat a lot of dry bones, hyenas need little water.
Gestation: 3 months. Usually bear 2-4 cubs.
Lifespan: 25 years

Spotted hyenas are mainly found in Lake Mburo, Queen Elizabeth as well as Mgahinga Forest national parks.

MONGOOSE
Cercopithecus ascarius

The species found in Uganda include; Egyptian mongoose, Marsh mongoose, Slender mongoose, White tailed mongoose, Banded Mongoose.

Habits: Mongoose are highly sociable and live in large troops - typically between 5 and 30 individuals.
Diet: Insects and other invertebrates, birds and their eggs, reptiles, small rodents, carrion, and snakes.
Gestation: 60 days, give birth to between 2 – 6 young.
Lifespan: 8 years

Ten species of mongoose have been recorded in Uganda with the banded mongoose regularly seen around the Mweya peninsular in Queen Elizabeth National Park as well as Kidepo Valley National Park.

WARTHOG
Phacochonoerus africanus

Neither graceful nor beautiful, Warthogs are nonetheless remarkable animals. As part of their grooming they take sand baths, rub against trees and termite mounds or let tickbirds pick insects off their bodies.

Habits: Warthogs live in family groups of a female and her young. Males normally live by themselves, only joining the female groups to mate.
Diet: The warthog is mainly a grazer and has an interesting practice of kneeling on its padded knees to eat short grass.
Gestation: 5 months, usually 4 piglets. Each has its 'own' teat and suckles exclusively from it. If one dies, others do not suckle from available teat.
Lifespan: 15 years.
Population: 3,686

Mainly found in Lake Mburo, Queen Elizabeth and Murchison Falls National parks and Kafu River basin.

GIANT HOG
Hylochocrus meinertzhageru

The slate-grey skin is densely covered with extremely coarse dark brown or black hair, although this becomes sparser with age. Forming a slight mane on the neck which is erected when excited, these hairs may grow to be 17cm long. Males are significantly larger than females in both weight and dimensions.

Habits: They live in groups. Activity is highest in the early morning and again in the late afternoon. Wallowing is a favourite activity, taking up about one hour each day in certain areas. Males are responsible for the defense of the group, and will attack objects which threaten the safety. Extremely fierce when excited, and will attack humans if they are shot at.
Diet: mainly grasses, roots, fruit, leaves, carrion.
Gestation: 149-154 days, give birth to 2-6, rarely up to 11. Females reach sexual maturity at one year, males at 3-4 years.
Lifespan: 12 years.

Found in nearly all the national parks in the country.

RED-RIVER HOG
Potamochoerus porcus

The shaggy, foxy red coat has contrasting black and white markings on the head, including a white eye ring. The body is round and is supported by short, sturdy legs. The upper tusks are relatively small and almost invisible, while the lower ones are razor-sharp and grow 7 cm or 3 inches long. They live in groups; sounders of 2-15 females and youngs, attended by a male.

Habits: Red river hogs are most active during the night, resting in a self-excavated burrow deep within impenetrable vegetation during the day. Red river hogs are fast runners and good swimmers. They often root for tubers with their plow-like noses and can cause considerable damage to crops in a short period of time.

Diet: Grasses, water plants, roots, bulbs, fruit, carrion, small animals.
Gestation: 120-127 days, giving birth to 1-4 piglets. It reaches sexual maturity at 18-21 months.
Lifespan: 20 years.

Found in nearly all the national parks in Uganda.

NILE CROCODILE
Crocodylus niloticus

It is one of the largest living reptiles. The Nile Crocodile can grow up to the length of six metres.

Habits: Lives in water; mostly near lake shores and rivers. A large crocodile is capable of killing a lion or an adult human being; it drowns its prey first, stores it under a tree until it is decomposed for easy eating.
Diet: Swimming mammals are their prey but basically feed on fish and young hippos.
Gestation: 8 months, laying 30-60 eggs.
Lifespan: 50 years in the wild, 80-100 years in captivity.

Nile crocodile is more confined to protected areas. They are seen on River Nile banks and also around Lake Mburo and Kazinga channel in Queen Elizabeth National Park.

NILE MONITOR LIZARD
Varanus niloticus

The Nile Monitor lizard is the largest lizard in Africa. Because they eat crocodile eggs, Nile monitors are often seen near crocodile nesting sites. Adult Nile Monitor lizards can easily outrun people over short distances. They can also remain underwater for more than an hour. The female Nile monitor lays her clutch of eggs in the active mounds of termites. The heat from the termites acts to incubate the eggs.

Habits: Generally live in rivers, water bodies; all over Africa except the northwest.

Diet: Fish, crocodile eggs, insects, aquatic creatures, and some mammals.

Lifespan: 15 years

RAINBOW (AGAMA) LIZARD
Agama agama

African Agama lizards are generally large and very colourful. The more common species in Uganda is the beautiful Rock Agama or Rainbow Lizard. Males reach over a foot (30 cm) long and sport bright orange, blue and brown colours.

Habits: Mostly docile except for a cock that defends his territory. There are several identifiable behaviours (head nod, head bob, challenge display, threat display, fighting, and basking). Sexual success determines the intensity of colours. For the prize of a harem of females, males fight one another. The winners are always startlingly bright but the defeated males turn out a dull grey, similar to the females.

Reproduction: When a female first approaches a male will bob his head and show his bright throat. If female is receptive the pair mate. Females lay 3 - 10 eggs, hatching in 8 to 10 weeks.

Diet: Omnivore – ants, grasshoppers, beetles, and termites. Though primarily an insectivore, the agama will eat small mammals, reptiles, and vegetation if necessary.

Lifespan: 6 – 10 years

RWENZORI THREE-HORNED CHAMELEON
Chamaeleo deremensis

Usually various shades of green, with dark and light swirls and bars. Conspicuous sail-like dorsal ridge. Males with three sharp horns.

Habits: Poorly known. Males probably use horns for combat. They live mostly in forest and woodland in fairly high elevation.
Diet: Feeds primarily on grasshoppers and beetles.

TORTOISE

The tortoise is a land-dwelling reptile. Like their aquatic cousins, the turtles, tortoises are shielded from predators by a shell. The carapace (top of shell) can help indicate the age of the tortoise by the number of concentric rings. Males tend to have a longer, protruding neck plate than their female counterparts.

Habits: Tortoises are generally reclusive and shy. Most land-based tortoises are herbivores, feeding on grazing grasses, weeds, leafy greens, flowers, and certain fruits.

Reproduction: 90-120 days to incubate from ping-pong-ball-sized eggs. Female tortoises dig and lay about a dozen eggs in holes they dig. Most hatchlings are born with an embryonic egg sac, serving as a source of food for the first couple of days.

Lifespan: Tortoises generally have lifespans comparable with those of human beings, and some individuals are known to have lived longer than 150 years.

CAPE HARE
Lepus capensis

The Cape Hare has long, round-tipped ears and a short fluffy tail which is black on top, white below and along the sides. The upper body is brownish yellow flecked with black and the throat and belly are white. Unlike with rabbits, hares' hind legs are considerably longer than their forelegs.

Habits: Hares are solitary and sedentary while rabbits are social. They are primarily nocturnal which is why they are commonly seen at night along roadsides. They keep their fur clean by regular grooming and dust-bathing. Unlike rabbits, hares do not excavate burrows, preferring to lie up in a form of flattened vegetation.

Diet: Primarily grass, although they also eat buds, twigs, bark, fungi, fruit and berries.

Gestation: 6 weeks

Lifespan: 3 years

They are found in open grasslands, light bushes and shrubs all over the country.

GROUND SQUIRREL
Spermophilus xerus

Ground squirrels and tree squirrels are different. You can tell the difference this way. Ground squirrels will run to their burrow in the ground if they are scared. Tree squirrels will climb a tree or high building.

Habits: Ground squirrels are mostly active during the day time. They spend a lot of their time underground in homes called burrows where they sleep, raise their babies, store food, and stay away from danger. When they dig their burrows, they make large hills of dirt and rock that buries grass or small plants.
Diet: Squirrels mainly eat grasses, seeds, grains, and nuts. They store food in their dens, too. They eat vegetables and field crops when they are first starting to grow.

HEDGEHOG
Aceleris albiventris

Hedgehogs have powerful legs and strong claws and are good at digging. They can run up to 6.5 ft/sec, but usually move with a slow shambling walk.

Habits: Mostly active at dawn and dusk. Can undergo periods of dormancy during which body temperature is drops to a level close to that of surrounding air. This reduces energy needs, allowing it to survive long periods.

Diet: Hedgehogs eat virtually any available invertebrate. They also eat seeds, berries or fallen fruit.

Gestation: 35-40 days. There is no pair bond formed and the male shows no paternal behaviour.

Lifespan: 8-10 years in captivity.

LARGE-EARED GREATER GALAGO (GREATER BUSHBABY)
Galago crassicaudatus

Similar in size to a small cat, the Greater Galago has large eyes, prominent ears and a bushy tail – which is carried erect like a cat's when it is moving. Greater Galagos are very noisy at night, particularly during the breeding season. The most commonly heard call is like that of a baby crying (hence the name bushbaby) and may may be repeated 50-100 times per hour, helping space individuals and acting as a contact call.

Habits: Exclusively nocturnal, the Galago inhabits woodlands, evergreen forests and savannah. It is solitary or lives in small family groups of adult female and their offspring.
Diet: Mainly fruit, seeds, flowers, nectar, gum, grubs and insects. They also eat small reptiles, birds' eggs and nestlings.
Gestation: 4 to 4¼ months. Galagos give birth to a single young though twins are also common.
Lifespan: 8 to 10 years.

Galagos are found in almost all of Uganda's national parks. In Lake Mburo National Park, their cries are common experience near Mihingo Lodge. The Senegal Galago, which is smaller, is common in Kidepo Valley National Park.

OTTER
Lutra maculicollis

The species identified in Uganda is the darker spotted-necked otter.

Habits: The otter is sociable, living in groups of 6-10 animals. They are very active between dusk and dawn when they hunt. They are nocturnal.

Diet: It feeds on crabs, fish and frogs

Gestation: 2 months. Along Lake Victoria, they usually pair in July and give birth in September.

These aquatic predators are associated with most wetlands and appear in some areas in Lake Mburo National Park.

Your checklist of animals in Uganda

Primates

1. Angolan (Rwenzori) Colobus, *Colobus anogolensis* ☐   Date: _____   Location: _____

2. Baboon, *Papio anubis* ☐   Date: _____   Location: _____

3. Black-and-white Colobus Monkey, *Colobus guereza* ☐   Date: _____   Location: _____

4. Blue Monkey, *Cercopithecus mitis* ☐   Date: _____   Location: _____

5. Chimpanzee, *Pan troglodytes* ☐   Date: _____   Location: _____

6. De Brazza's Monkey, *Cercopithecus neglectus* ☐   Date: _____   Location: _____

7. Grey-cheeked Mangabey, *Cercocebus albigena* ☐   Date: _____   Location: _____

8. L'hoest's Monkey, *cercopithecus l'hoesti* ☐   Date: _____   Location: _____

9. Mountain Gorilla *Gorilla gorilla* ☐   Date: _____   Location: _____

10. Patas Monkey, *erythrocebus patas* ☐   Date: _____   Location: _____

11. Red Colobus Monkey, *procobus badius* ☐   Date: _____   Location: _____

12. Red-Tailed Monkey, *cercopithecus ascarius* ☐   Date: _____   Location: _____

13. Vervet Monkey, *cercopithecus aethiops* ☐   Date: _____   Location: _____

Large Mammals

1. Buffalo, *Syncerus caffer* ☐   Date: _____   Location: _____

2. Elephant, *Loxodonta africana* ☐   Date: _____   Location: _____

3. Giraffe *Giraffa camelorpardalis* ☐   Date: _____   Location: _____

4. Hippopotamus, *Hippoptamus amphibius* ☐   Date: _____   Location: _____

5. Rhinoceros *Ceratotherium simum* ☐   Date: _____   Location: _____

Horned Ungulates (antelopes)

1. Bohor Reedbuck, *Redunca redunca* ☐   Date: _____   Location: _____

2. Bushbuck, *Tragelaphus scriptus* ☐   Date: _____   Location: _____

3. Duiker ☐   Date: _____   Location: _____

4. Eland, *Taurotragus oryx* ☐   Date: _____   Location: _____

5. Impala, *Aepytceros melampus* ☐   Date: _____   Location: _____

6. Grant's Gazelle ☐   Date: _____   Location: _____

7. Greater Kudu *Tregelaphus strepsiceros* ☐   Date: _____   Location: _____

8. Guenther's Dik-dik *Madoqua guentheri* ☐   Date: _____   Location: _____

9. Hartebeest *Alcelaphus buselaphus* ☐   Date: _____   Location: _____

10. Klipspringer *Oroetragus oreotragus* ☐   Date: _____   Location: _____

11. Lesser Kudu *Tregelaphus imberbis* ☐   Date: _____   Location: _____

12. Mountain Reedbuck *Redunca fulvorufula* ☐   Date: _____   Location: _____

13. Oribi, *Ourebia ourebia* ☐   Date: _____   Location: _____

14. Oryx (*Oryx gazelle*) BELIEVED TO BE EXTINCT ☐   Date: _____   Location: _____

15. Pygmy Antelope *Neofragus batesi* ☐   Date: _____   Location: _____

16. Roan Antelope *Hippotragus equines* ☐   Date: _____   Location: _____

17. Sitatunga *Tragelaphus spekii* ☐   Date: _____   Location: _____

18. Topi *Damaliscus lunatus* ☐   Date: _____   Location: _____

19. Uganda Kob *Kobus kob* ☐   Date: _____   Location: _____

20. Waterbuck *Kobus ellipsiprymnus* ☐   Date: _____   Location: _____

21. Zebra, *Equus burchelli* ☐   Date: _____   Location: _____

Cats

1. Cheetah, *Acinonyx jubatus* ☐   Date: _____   Location: _____
2. African Golden Cat, *Felis aurata* ☐   Date: _____   Location: _____
3. Caracal, *Felis caracal* ☐   Date: _____   Location: _____
4. African Wild Cat *Felis silvestris* ☐   Date: _____   Location: _____
5. Lion *Panthera leo* ☐   Date: _____   Location: _____
6. Leopard *Panthera pardus* ☐   Date: _____   Location: _____
7. Serval *Felis serval* ☐   Date: _____   Location: _____

Hogs

Giant Hog *Hylochocrus meinertzhageru* ☐   Date: _____   Location: _____
Red-River Hog *Potamochoerus porcus* ☐   Date: _____   Location: _____
Warthog *Phacochonoerus africanus* ☐   Date: _____   Location: _____

Dogs, Jackals & Foxes

1. Golden Jackal, *Canis aureus* ☐   Date: _____   Location: _____
2. Black-backed Jackal, *Canis mesomelas* ☐   Date: _____   Location: _____
3. Hunting Dog (African Wild), *Lyacaon pictus* ☐   Date: _____   Location: _____
4. Bat-eared Fox, *Otocyon megalotis* ☐   Date: _____   Location: _____
5. Hunting Dog (Wild Dog), *Lycaon pictus* ☐   Date: _____   Location: _____
6. Jackal, *Lerus adustus* ☐   Date: _____   Location: _____

Weasels, Badgers & Otters

1. African Clawless Otter, *Aonyx capensis* ☐   Date: _____   Location: _____

2. Congo Clawless Otter, *Aonyx congica* ☐   Date: _____   Location: _____

3. Zorilla (Striped Polecat), *Ictonyx striatus* ☐   Date: _____   Location: _____

4. Honey Badger (Ratel), *Mellivora capensis* ☐   Date: _____   Location: _____

5. East African Striped Weasel, *Poecilogale albinucha*   Date: _____   Location: _____

6. Otter, *Lutra maculicollis* ☐   Date: _____   Location: _____

Civets & Genets

1. East African Civet, *Civetttictis civetta* ☐   Date: _____   Location: _____

2. Small-spotted Genet, *Genetta genetta* ☐   Date: _____   Location: _____

3. Servaline Genet, *Genetta servalina* ☐   Date: _____   Location: _____

4. Rusty Spotted Genet, *Genetta tigrina* ☐   Date: _____   Location: _____

5. Giant Forest Genet, *Genetta victoriae* ☐   Date: _____   Location: _____

6. African Pal Civet, *Nandinia binotata* ☐   Date: _____   Location: _____

7. Aquatic Genet, *Osbornictus piscivora* ☐   Date: _____   Location: _____

Mongooses

1. Marsh Mongoose, *Atilax paludinosus* ☐   Date: _____   Location: _____

2. Jackson's Mongoose, *Bdeogale jacksoni* ☐   Date: _____   Location: _____

3. Alexander's Cusimanse/Dark Mongoose, *Crossarchus alexandri* ☐ Date: _____   Location: _____

4. Savanna Mongoose, *Dologale dybowskii* ☐   Date: _____   Location: _____

5. Desert Dwarf Mongoose, *Helogale parvula* ☐   Date: _____   Location: _____

6. Egyptian Mongoose, *Herpestes ichneumon* ☐   Date: _____   Location: _____

7. Slender Mongoose, *Herpestes sanguineus* ☐   Date: _____   Location: _____

8. White-tailed Mongoose, *Ichneumia albicauda* ☐   Date: _____   Location: _____

9. Banded Mongoose, *Mungos mungo* ☐   Date: _____   Location: _____

10. Mongoose, *Cercopithecus ascarius* ☐   Date: _____   Location: _____

Ardwolf & Hyenas

1. Striped Hyena, *Hyaena hyaena* ☐   Date: _____   Location: _____

2. Aardwolf, *Proteles cristatus* ☐   Date: _____   Location: _____

3. Hyena, *Crocuta crocuta* ☐   Date: _____   Location: _____

Pangolins

1. Giant Pangolin, *Manis gigantea* ☐   Date: _____   Location: _____

2. Ground Pangolin, *Manis temmincki* ☐   Date: _____   Location: _____

3. Long-tailed Pangolin, *Manis tetrdactyla* ☐   Date: _____   Location: _____

4. Tree Pangolin, *Manis tricuspis* ☐   Date: _____   Location: _____

Squirrels

1. Beecroft's Flying Squirrel, *Anomalurus beecrofti* ☐   Date: _____   Location: _____

2. Lord Derby's Flying Squirrel, *Anomalurus derbianus* ☐   Date: _____   Location: _____

3. African Dwarf Flying Squirrel, *Idiurus zenkeri* ☐   Date: _____   Location: _____

4. Ground Squirrel, *Spermophilus xerus* ☐   Date: _____   Location: _____

Porcupines

1. Brush-tailed Porcupine, *Atherurus africanus* ☐   Date: _____   Location: _____
2. South African Porcupine, *Hystrix africae-australis* ☐   Date: _____   Location: _____
3. Crested Porcupine, *Hystrix cristata* ☐   Date: _____   Location: _____

Hares

1. Cape (Brown) Hare, *Lepus capensis* ☐   Date: _____   Location: _____
2. Savanna (Crawshay's) Hare, *Lepus victoriae* ☐   Date: _____   Location: _____
3. Bunyoro Rabbit, *Poelagus marjorita* ☐   Date: _____   Location: _____

Reptiles

1. Nile Crocodile, *Crocodylus niloticus* ☐   Date: _____   Location: _____
2. Nile Monitor lizard, *Varanus niloticus* ☐   Date: _____   Location: _____
3. Rainbow Lizard, *Agama agama* ☐   Date: _____   Location: _____
4. Rwenzori Three-horned Chameleon, *Chamaeleo deremensis* ☐   Date: _____   Location: _____

Others

Hedgehog, *Aceleris albiventris* ☐   Date: _____   Location: _____

Large-Eared greater Galago (greater bush-baby), *Galago crassicaudatus* ☐ Date: _____ Location: _____

English name	Swahili	Luganda	Luo	Atesot	Lusoga
Agama Lizard		Konkome	Agwegwe	Eidodo	Omudholome
Baboon	Nyani		Bim/Abim		Ensudhe
Bat		Kawundo	Olik	Eminia	Kawundhowundo
Buffalo	Nyati	Mbogo	Jobi		Embogo
Bush Buck	Pongo	Ngabi			Engabi
Chameleon	Kigeugeu	Nawolovu	Agogongo/Agogo	Agoogo	Akakanyavu
Cheetah	Duma	Njaza	Kworo		Endhaza
Chimpanzee	Sokwe mtu	Zzike	Bim/Abim	Emabworo	Eirike
Dik dik	Funo		Amor		
Duiker		Ntalaganya	Amor		
Eland	Pofu				
Elephant	Ndovu	Njovu	Lyech	Etome	Endovu
Frog/Toad	Chura	Kikere	Ogwalogwal	Aidodok	Ekikere
Giraffe	Twiga	Ntuga	Riho/Rio	Akale	Entwiiga
Grant's Gazelle	Swala Granti		Anyem		
Hartebeest	Nkonze				
Hippopotamus	Kiboko	Nvubu	Imir/Raho/Rao	Emiria	Envubu
Hog		Emizi yomunsiko	Punu lum		Embidhi edhomunsiko
Hunting/Wild Dog	Mbwa Mwitu	Mbwa	Ipee		
Hyena	Fisi	Mpisi	Odyek	Ebuu	Empiti
Impala	Swala	Mpala			Empongo

Runyankore/Rukiga	Runyoro/Rutooro	Lugisu/Lumasaba	Lusamia	Lugbara
Ekihangare	Munya		Ehohome	Olokoto
Enkobe	Nkerebe		Enguke	Ojimata
Akahundu	Kihuguhugu	Mawugutu	Embudobudo	Bibia
Embogo	Mbogo		Emboko	Odru
Engabi				
Enyaruju			Ehaniafu	Indrekindre
Ekyoha				Odoo
	Kikuya			Ngbeleke
				Ndire
Ekishwaga				
Enjojo	Njojo	Inzhofu	Enjofu	Ewa
Ekikyere	Kikere		Ehere	Udruata
	Twiga		Njaya mutumba	Oteleke
				Oboa
Enjubu	Nsere		Efubu	Robi
Empunu		Imbitsi	Embichi yo musino	
Omushega				Andalaka
Empitsi	Mpisi	Namunyu	Engu	Obawu
Empala			Embongo	Ebba

English name	Swahili	Luganda	Luo	Atesot	Lusoga
Jackal	Mbweha nyukundu	Kibe	Ikwe	Ekuwe	Ekibe
Klipspringer	Mbuzi Mawe				
Leopard	Chui	Ngo	Kwach	Erisa	Empala
Lion	Simba	Mpologoma	Abwor/Ingato	Ekosobwan	Empologoma
Mongoose	Nguchiro	Kakolwa	Ogwangweno/Gor	Icuuli	
Monitor Lizard		Nswaswa	Ngec/Ngengec	Egengeri	Embulu
Monkey - Colobus	Mbega	Ngeye	Dolo		
Monkey - Patas	Kima				
Monkey - Vervet	Tumbili	Nkima	Ajam/Ayom	Edokolet	Nkembo
Mt.Gorilla	N'gagi				
Nile Crocodile	Mamba	Goonya	Nyanyang/Nyang	Akinganga	Engoihna
Otter		Ng'onge	Ongonge		
Rhinoceros	Kifaru	Nkula	Amuka		
Serval	Mondo	Emmondo	Kworo	Atawoi	Emondho
Sitatunga	Nzohe		Imali		
Squirrel		Nkerebwe	Ayita	Ikunyuk	Kadhadha
Uganda Kob			Til	Akale	Empongo
Warthog	Ngiri	Njiri	Kul		Enkula
Waterbuck	Kuro				
Zebra	Punda Milia	Ntulege	Ekori/Etuku		Entulege